# *The Prestige*
# North We

## John Banks
## Photography by G H F Atkins

© 2001 J M Banks & G H F Atkins

ISBN 1 898432 27 9

*Cover:* A Tilling-Stevens in colour in an artist's impression from North Western's May 1931 timetable. *(Keith Healey Collection)*

*Inside front cover:* The North Western territory was already extensive in 1928, when the timetable from which this map is taken was published. *(Keith Healey Collection)*

*Inside rear cover:* Towards the end of the Company's separate existence timetables still had artist's impressions of buses on the front. This 1962 example cost 9d. *(Keith Healey Collection)*

*Rear cover:* A typically fine prewar timetable leaflet. As so often with these publications the drawing of the single-decker is somewhat stylised. *(Keith Healey Collection)*

*Title page:* Geoffrey Atkins would organise a day out with the camera in the Manchester area around a train journey from Nottingham to Manchester. On occasion he would take a bus down the A6 into Stockport to record the North Western fleet in its headquarters town. This view dates from May 1952 and was taken from the A6 as it passes through the centre of Stockport. The famous railway viaduct forms a backcloth to the bus parking area that is the location, a half-century on, of Stockport's bus station. The North Western fleet is represented by a Weymann-bodied Leyland Titan and a trio of Bristol L5Gs with Eastern Coach Works bodywork.

*Opposite page:* Lower Mosley Street coach station was always on the itinerary when the photographer was in Manchester. Right up to the disappearance of North Western into SELNEC (and beyond for a while) the Company's vehicles in the traditional livery were there in quantity on a variety of local and express services. Among the most attractive of contemporary coaches were some Duple Northern-bodied 41-seat Leyland Leopards delivered in 1968. These supremely comfortable vehicles are represented by No. **257 (KJA257F)** photographed alongside a Ribble coach in April 1972: by then North Western had become part of SELNEC, a change which had taken place in January 1972.

*Below:* Stockport again, this time in April 1954. The line of buses gives a useful cross-section of the contemporary fleet: an Atkinson underfloor-engined single-decker, prewar rebodied and postwar Bristol single-deckers and a rebodied Guy Arab double-decker.

PRIVATE 123

KJA257F

NORTH WESTERN

## INTRODUCTION

As the new millennium begins, the writer's High Street, in Romiley, Cheshire, looks like that of many another small village swallowed up by the march of twentieth-century suburbanisation (in this case that of Stockport, itself these days effectively an extension of Manchester); the many small shops and myriad shoppers are threaded by the garishly liveried single- and double-deckers of the Stagecoach fleet leavened with those - scarcely less garish - of one or two brave independents. Looking back, from the vantage point of that wonderland situated halfway between sleeping and wakefulness, it is possible to hear, passing the end of the street not fifty yards away, Bristol Js and Ks with growling Gardners, lumbering Leylands, not to mention the odd archaic-looking Tilling-Stevens, on the way to Greave, Compstall, Marple or Mellor. These fine vehicles had a smart, traditional livery of red and cream with the fleetname NORTH WESTERN and, of course, in common with numerous other much-missed bus fleets of yore, they represent in the mind's eye something that no longer exists.

Readers who have followed the writer's reminiscing in earlier volumes of the *Prestige Series* will recall the way in which he, as a small boy, became aware of certain fleets in his home town (Hull Corporation and East Yorkshire) and how visits (usually, but mercifully not always, under parental or school control) to foreign parts within a not very large radius of Hull brought discoveries such as Lincolnshire, United and West Yorkshire. Other operators were glimpsed in passing, so to speak, and writing in this series about such fleets as Yorkshire Traction, Yorkshire Woollen and East

Midland evoked many a memory of frustrated enthusiasm when vehicles, bus stations and depots flashed past the windows of the parental motor car.

London Transport, of course, was in a category all by itself. All small boys, even those who had not been within hundreds of miles of it, knew that there was a Capital, that it was called London, and that it had a vast fleet of trams, trolleybuses, buses and coaches to serve its population. "Ten million people" was the figure always quoted in geography lessons and to the writer's recollection the only information about public transport ever volunteered by a teacher in a school lesson was when the size of the London Transport fleet was evoked, in the same breath as the establishment strength of the Metropolitan Police, to show what enormous resources (ten thousand and twenty thousand respectively were the figures somewhat inaccurately quoted; numbers beyond the comprehension, if truth be told, of small boys living in a city of a mere three hundred thousand souls needing a combined bus fleet numbered in the lower hundreds) were required by the Capital's teeming millions.

From the North Western operating area, of such places as Stockport, Macclesfield, and even Manchester, such grubby schoolboy bus spotters recked little (although the latter was mentioned in class as being an important port, despite its distance from the sea, so at least we had heard of it). Buxton and Matlock, however, were, as indeed they still are, attractive tourist destinations and each was visited perhaps twice during the writer's schooldays. But of the buses there, not a shred of memory remains. Thus this look at North Western becomes the first in the *Prestige Series* not to have its *potpourri* of

4

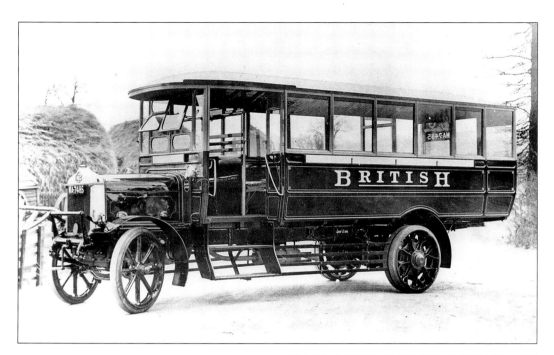

*Above: A 1921 AEC, No. **391** (**MA7485**), of the BRITISH fleet, which became No. 43 upon the formation of the North Western Road Car Company Limited. (Geoffrey Atkins Collection)*

*Right: An early, pre-North Western timetable. (Keith Healey Collection)*

experiences culled from the writer's formative years.

Later, it was different. Transplanted to London and gainfully employed, he gravitated to Victoria coach station and noted, among vast riches hitherto unimagined by a former denizen of a provincial backwater, the coaches of North Western. (In retrospect, it is remarkable how many fleets were encountered for the first time through their express coach operations witnessed many miles from their less glamorous stage carriage areas: East Kent, Thames Valley, Southdown, Maidstone & District, Western SMT and Eastern Scottish and so on; not to mention that artist's palette of Black & White, Royal Blue, Midland Red, with Yelloway, Grey-Green and Orange Luxury sometimes working on hire at busy times... Ah, one could write a book!)

The North Western Road Car Company Limited, of Stockport, traced its beginnings to 1913: thus it was born in the earliest days of mechanised passenger services. North Western was a profitable and successful company right up to the bitter end when its enforced demise (for political rather than operational reasons)

THE

# BRITISH

AUTOMOBILE TRACTION CO. LTD.

## MACCLESFIELD & BUXTON DISTRICT.

## Time Table

### August 1st, 1920
And until further notice.

*North Western's traditional fleetname transfer contrasts with the aggressively modern - for the era - Leyland Royal Tiger badge on one of the Weymann-bodied machines. (John Senior)*

Local authorities were less enthusiastic, however, and there was an obstructive attitude over licensing. Then the First World War vehicle requisitioning programme robbed the fledgling operation of its best Daimler vehicles. This all made for slow progress. Things improved after a show of protest from ratepayers and after the war a decent fleet of AECs and Daimlers was built up. Services in Stockport and the Peak District spa town of Buxton were begun and by the beginning of the 1920s the fleet numbered some 30 vehicles. In 1921 Glossop was reached.

saw it subsumed into one of the new Passenger Transport Executives - SELNEC (South East Lancashire North East Cheshire) - in 1972. In the intervening 60 years the Company built up a reputation as a provider of an excellent standard of comfort, reliability, courtesy and punctuality seldom surpassed by its contemporaries and never by its unwieldy successors of whatever livery (both actual and political). North Western was perhaps the ideal operator. Its fleet size was manageable: neither too large nor too small; its maintenance standards were high; its management was first class and - perhaps most importantly - all levels of staff were proud of the Company and intensely loyal to it. This excellence was, in the normal run of everyday operations, manifestly present (in those days it did not need the "evidence" of either a vogueish British Standard number or a framed certificate on the wall) and the travelling public responded.

Back in 1913 that confusing parent and offspring team, the British Electric Traction Company Limited and the British Automobile Traction Company Limited (the latter was a subsidiary of the former) pursued a policy, where the BET had no tramway operation, of assessing whether motor-bus services might be commercially viable and, if so, of the BAT introducing one or more. Thus, in the Cheshire town of Macclesfield, at the end of 1913, "British" buses began to run to great enthusiasm on the part of the local populace.

These services and those at Barrow-in-Furness were the only BAT operations outside London and when in 1922 the Barrow branch closed, the expanding Macclesfield and Peak District services were thought in need of some administrative reassessment and the Peak District Committee was formed. This resulted in the introduction of money from Thomas Tilling Limited and the formation of a separate company. Thus, on 23rd April 1923, the North Western Road Car Company Limited was registered.

The new company had a fleet of over 50 vehicles and, in 1924, its headquarters was moved to Charles Street, Stockport - an address still prominent in the Stagecoach portfolio. Tilling and BAT each had a 50% stake in North Western, which not unnaturally led to heavy investment in Tilling-Stevens chassis, in the manufacture of which Tilling was directly involved. Thus, in its first five years, North Western bought 280, including double-deckers. The earlier examples had petrol-electric transmission, which was much smoother than clutch and mechanical transmission. These latter improved, however, as the decade progressed and eventually consigned petrol-electrics to virtual oblivion.

As the 1920s drew to a close, the administrative history of the Company began to follow the familiar path whereby a new holding company named Tilling and British Automobile Traction Company Limited assumed control of

*A selection of North Western Bell Punch tickets. The Company had various other types of ticket-issuing equipment, notably Willebrew. (Keith Healey Collection)*

all the shares in the NWRCC; then, following legislation which allowed the railway companies to involve themselves in road transport, the LMS and the LNE Railways jointly acquired a 49.8% shareholding in North Western. The BET also had 49.8; the remaining small percentage was in private hands.

Nineteen-twenty-nine and the early 1930s brought a swing to Leyland chassis, although the last Tilling-Stevens - which was the 431st - came as late as March 1932. Dennis chassis were also bought as the thirties progressed, and then the Bristol (by then under Tilling control) became the fleet standard until such chassis could no longer be bought following the 1947 Transport Act nationalisation scheme which materialised the following year. North Western had gone into the BET camp at the time of the 1942 split into BET and Tilling companies, and was therefore precluded from placing orders with Bristol after nationalisation.

Many independent operators were bought out by North Western from its earliest years with the obvious advantages that reduced competition brought; further positive moves were operating agreements concluded with a number of municipal and company operators including the famous and long-lasting 1928 "by arrangement" agreement with Manchester Corporation which survived for more than four decades.

The postwar years saw a rather remarkable rebodying programme in which scores of chassis were refurbished and fitted with new bodies; the latter in some cases were used on more than one chassis as the older chassis finally wore out and were withdrawn. Administrative expansion continued after the war, too, and in 1958 the share capital of two

substantial independents, Altrincham Coachways and Melba Motors, was acquired. In an interesting move, standard North Western vehicles were drafted in to replace the Altrincham and Melba fleets. The separate identity of these subsidiaries was maintained for almost a decade; then, in 1967, Melba was absorbed into North Western and Altrincham Coachways was sold.

On 1st January 1969 the National Bus Company began its existence. This had been preceded, made possible indeed, by the earlier negotiations which saw the BET sell all its United Kingdom bus business to the Transport Holding Company. North Western had been part of the BET empire, and was now quietly swallowed up into the NBC. Later, in 1972, as we have seen, it became the Cheshire arm of the SELNEC PTE; North Western stage services outside the PTE area were sold to other NBC operators. North Western itself survived purely as an NBC coach operator.

The operation of bus services is a very serious business but it has had its humorous side. Any large bus operator's staff invariably had its share of characters and comedians; North Western was no exception. Such matters are not usually reported in serious works about the industry. But North Western was such a uniquely "family" operation that the following reminiscences, based on tales told by employees who, in 1948, had completed over 25 years service with North Western and British, will serve as a lighter-than-usual-hearted end to our look at this much-missed operator.

The most common misfortune was to lose a wheel. Charlie Mellor recalled his first night as a conductor on the Macclesfield to Cheadle service when one of the rear wheels came off. Charlie had to make himself comfortable in the driver's seat to keep the engine running whilst the driver went for assistance. He leant his elbow on the rubber tube leading from the acetylene generator and extinguished the lights. When he realised what had happened he moved his elbow, released the pressure and turned the interior of the bus into a gas chamber. The passengers were not amused.

Joe Lomas lost a wheel one winter when the snow was windswept high over the hedges. The wheel was shod with a solid tyre, it rolled to the top of the bank, came to rest near the top and, on an even keel, rolled gracefully back again.

Gordon Henshaw operating the Stockport to Hayfield service did not realise he had lost a rear wheel until it overtook him, his bus continuing the while on three wheels.

Charlie Mellor also suffered being blown off the top of his bus while walking across the roof to relight the tail lamp which was placed very high on the vehicle. If you didn't have a match to relight the acetylene lamps, you had to climb the nearest gas-lamp post for a light.

Albert Higginbotham recalled occasions when he had as many as fifteen passengers crammed into the driver's cab, others riding on the wings and some even sitting on top. Other drivers have stated that it was not uncommon to carry passengers sitting back-to-back in the luggage space on the roof of single-deckers, gained by climbing the ladder fixed at the rear or, in the case of some early buses, at the front of the bus.

Whilst travelling from Buxton to Stockport a satisfied passenger sitting beside the driver, Gordon Henshaw, gave him a tip - three certainties at a race meeting. Gordon and pals backed all three. They won at excellent odds: two at 10-1, the other at 100-8.

Some of Frank Carter's experiences on private hire work are also worth recalling. Having taken a party to New Brighton his charabanc broke down on the return journey in Delamere Forest and he found that the carburettor jets had gone. Being resourceful he went in search of suitable twigs to improvise some temporary jets. Meanwhile a collection was made amongst the passengers for Frank, When it got around that it came to 1/6fid, one gentleman, who had put 2/6d in the hat, became very annoyed and the collector's middle name became "Mud". The passengers took sides and a fight developed. Eventually the party arrived back in Macclesfield at 3am having travelled home on carburettor jets made of tiny twigs with holes bored through them with the point of a very sharp penknife.

On another occasion whilst taking a party of clergymen from Leek to Lichfield Cathedral it started to rain and Frank stopped to put the hood up. He tackled this job alone; kneeling on the back seat, he leaned over and was lifting the heavy hood nicely when one of the parsons remarked "Blessed are they that are strong for they shall have strength". At that moment Frank lost his grip, the hood flopped back and he landed among his passengers.

Harry Holland added a new concept to conducting when a lorry suddenly emerged from a side road and knocked the steps off the bus. Harry, not daunted, borrowed a pair of step ladders and carried on the service. Next morning he and his driver were complimented on their resourcefulness in keeping the service going. Today they would probably be sacked and prosecuted.

This has been neither a history nor a fleet list of North Western. We have ended on a note of humour as a tribute to the staff who made North Western what it was, and whose vehicles were so beautifully recorded on film by Geoffrey Atkins.

This publication owes much to the generous help of David and Mary Shaw, who have once again read the proofs; Ron Maybray, who has been his usual infallible self in identifying vehicles; John Senior and Keith Healey, who have read the draft with an expert's eye and made numerous suggestions which have much improved the book. Keith has in addition provided the North Western items which grace these introductory pages and the covers; much of Keith's collection is now deposited with the Greater Manchester Transport Society, who have courteously allowed the use of various items. The PSV Circle's fleet history of North Western has been invaluable, as have the two TPC volumes on North Western by Eric Ogden et al, for some of the information included in the captions. All are most warmly thanked.

Lastly: the commercial artists who drew for the covers of timetables and leaflets in years gone by deserve our thanks. Their work was ephemeral: or so they thought; today we find much pleasure in it and are glad that so much has survived for so long after its expiry date.

*John Banks*
*Romiley, Cheshire*
*February 2001*

*Above:* North Western's Tilling-Stevens chassis began to flood in in 1924. There had been some new Daimlers in 1923 - the year of North Western's inauguration - based on reconditioned ex-WD chassis dating from the war years, which were probably ordered by British. No fewer than 36 Tilling-Stevens TS6 models joined the fleet in 1924, clearly funded by the influx of capital from Thomas Tilling Ltd. They all - except for one Brush-bodied vehicle - had bodywork also by Tilling. Number **80 (DB5025)** was brand new when the picture was taken. Its body was semi-convertible, with full-drop windows and roll-back canvas covers.

*Below:* In a mere six years the advent of pneumatic tyres and a more cohesively styled body design wrought what today seems like much more than a half-decade's worth of modernisation. Progress was rapid, though, in those days, and whereas the 1924 vehicle could never have been mistaken for anything else - even then - Brush-bodied No. **448 (DB9348)** is already recognisable as the standard half-cab single-decker that was to last practically unchanged in its visual design parameters until the early 1950s. The bus was also brand new when photographed. These photographs, both bodybuilder's official views, were added to the photographer's collection to help fill in the gaps where he had personally missed recording various types.

Brush-bodied Tilling-Stevens B10A2 No. **555** (**DB9455**) of 1931 was caught by the photographer in a sunny Lower Mosley Street coach station, Manchester, in May 1935. The bus was exactly halfway through its short life with North Western, for it was withdrawn and sold to a scrap dealer in 1939.

*Above:* New Tilling-Stevens B10A2s were still appearing in North Western livery in 1932, though by then their ascendancy had been somewhat dented by Leyland Motors, who since 1929 had sold both single- and double-deckers into the North Western fleet. Number **605** (**JA2205**) was bodied by Tilling as a rear-entrance 31-seater. It was photographed in its first few months of service, in front of the LMS railway station in Sheffield. It was withdrawn in 1939.

*Below:* The only new vehicles in 1933 were six Leyland KP2 Cubs with Brush 20-seat front-entrance bodywork. This was another type that the photographer missed and his photograph of No. **620** (**JA2220**), the last of the batch, came from the coachbuilder.

*Above:* One of the earliest Leylands was No. **398** (**DB5298**), a 1929 Tiger TS1 fitted with a Leyland 26-seat rear-entrance bus body, which was effectively the bottom half of Leyland's standard double-deck body of the era. There were 15 of these TS1s, and they were all withdrawn in 1931 and sold to a London dealer. The photograph was taken at Huntingdon Street, Nottingham, in August 1929.

*<< Opposite page:* One of 1932's Leyland Tiger TS4s, No. **585** (**DB9485**), is seen at Oxford Road, Llandudno, in June 1933. The 32-seat rear-entrance coachwork was by Eastern Counties, of Lowestoft. Number 585 was a 1941 withdrawal when it was requisitioned by the Ministry of War Transport.

*Below:* Number **636** (**JA2236**) was a 1934 Dennis Lancet with Eastern Counties 31-seat bus bodywork. It was photographed in June 1934. This one lasted with North Western until 1946.

<< *Opposite page:* The Dennis/Eastern Counties combination also appeared in 1934 in the 20-seat service bus category in the shape of four Aces with front entrances. There were also two Harrington-bodied 20-seat Ace coaches; one of them, No. **656** (**JA2256**), was photographed in September 1934 on a tour at Alton Towers in Staffordshire. North Western's service bus version of the "Flying Pig", as the Ace was affectionately known, was one-man-operated. All six Dennis Aces were withdrawn in 1945.

*This page:* A prize-winning design of 32-seat coachwork from Harrington graced a dozen Leyland Tiger TS6s in the same year. The stepped window arrangement was possibly a little clumsy, but it was a bold design move for that era. Our pictures are of No. **662** (**JA2262**) *(above)* with gold-lined mudguards, in Parliament Street, Nottingham in August 1934, and No. **666** (**JA2266**) at Lower Mosley Street, Manchester *(below)* the previous June. Number 662 was operating on North Western's longest route, the 14-hour Liverpool to Lowestoft. Taken over from Ribble in 1933, this service ceased to operate in 1936.

*<< Opposite page:* "They don't make 'em like that any more." Trite, but nonetheless true for all that. This magnificent machine - a combination of Leyland Tiger TS7 chassis and the Harrington stepped-window design of 32-seat coach - was in Victoria coach station, London, in August 1936. It had been new earlier that year.

*Above:* The same coach - No. **720 (JA5520)** - with an almost exactly reversed livery, at Huntingdon Street, Nottingham in August 1948. Number 720 was rebodied as a coach by Windover in 1950 and lasted until 1957. One of these coaches survives in preservation.

*Below:* Twelve TS7 Tigers were bought in 1935, fitted with the Harrington half-canopy coach bodies. Before they entered service, the bodies were exchanged for the full-canopied versions, also by Harrington, on 1931's petrol-engined Tiger TS1s 504-515. This was apparently through a desire to have the newest coach bodies powered by the smoother petrol-engined chassis. As if that were not complicated anough, the 1935 chassis were rebodied by Eastern Coach Works in 1938 and then again by Weymann in 1948. Both rebodyings were as service buses: with 31 seats by ECW and 35 by Weymann; and when the TS7 chassis wore out, the bodies went onto Bristols. Number **677 (JA2277)**, at Huntingdon Street, Nottingham, in October 1951, demonstrates the Weymann incarnation. It was not particularly luxurious for the long and difficult run from Nottingham to Manchester via Matlock and Buxton, but it must have been an exhilarating run for the enthusiasts of either buses or scenery.

<< *Opposite page:* One of the first Bristols in the fleet, No. **729** (**JA5529**), was a JO5G with Eastern Coach Works 31-seat bus bodywork, delivered in 1936. In July of that year it was also on the Nottingham to Manchester run, labelled EXPRESS, which was a bit optimistic for Gardner five-cylinder power. Even though No. 729 made no claim to be anything other than a service bus, its seating was sumptuous and it was equipped with a side board proudly detailing the express route on which it was working. By then the words "Limited Stop" had been removed from the side boards for all services except the Tyne-Tees-Mersey, which was widely referred to as simply "the Limited Stop".

*This page:* Two of 1937's Leyland TS8 Tigers: No. **814** (**JA7714**) *(above)* with its original Harrington 32-seat coach body, and **JA7705** as rebodied by Windover in 1950, still as a 32-seat coach, and renumbered as No. **386**. It had been fleet number 805. The photographs were at Lower Mosley Street, Manchester in July 1953 and Huntingdon Street, Nottingham, in May 1951. Number 814 was withdrawn later in 1953; 386 with its new body lasted until 1957. The Windovers were withdrawn *en masse* after a comparatively minor accident to one of them revealed substantial body problems.

*This page:* There was a large intake of Bristols in 1938, including many L5G single-deckers with ECW 31-seat bodies, exemplified by No. **864 (JA7764)**, seen *(above)* at The Square, Buxton in August 1950. Number **869A (JA7769)** *(below)* was one of a number of the 1938 machines which in 1952 were lengthened and fitted with 7ft 9ins-wide Willowbrook 38-seat rear-entrance bodies. A low axle-ratio was specified for use on the hilly Matlock routes. The picture was taken at Lower Mosley Street, Manchester in July 1953.

>> *Opposite page:* AEC Rangers were never a common sight. This fine Duple-bodied 26-seat coach was a 1933 purchase by William Howe, of Stockport, in 1933. It was brand new when photographed at Llandudno in June 1933. Howe sold out in 1935 and **JA3504** became North Western's No. 171.

<< *Opposite page:* Here is the ex-Howe AEC Ranger, No. **171** (**JA3504**), in North Western livery and service at Huntingdon Street, Nottingham, in 1937. For such a non-standard vehicle, a withdrawal date of 1945 is rather surprising. It must have been worth keeping; belying, perhaps, the poor reputation enjoyed by the few Rangers that were built. JA3504 was sold to Purple Coaches (William Makinson), of Manchester, who used a picture of it on the front of their extended tours brochure. It operated seven-day tours to Torquay, where it would have been at home among the AEC Rangers in the Grey Cars fleet.

*This page:* The North Western rebodying programme in the postwar period became ever more complicated. Bristol L5G No. **673** (**AJA143**) of 1938 *(above)*, got its 1948 Weymann body and new fleet number from a prewar Leyland TS7 in 1953. AJA143 had originally been fleet number 943. Number 940 (**AJA140**) *(below)* was a straightforward 1951 rebodying by Burlingham. In this case a postwar PV2, lower-positioned radiator was fitted, much modernising the appearance and the bus was renumbered **376**. The pictures are at Lower Mosley Street, Manchester in July 1953 and The Square, Buxton, in August 1951.

*Above:* The 1938 Bristol K5Gs, originally equipped with Eastern Coach Works 47-seat lowbridge bodywork, were the first double-deckers bought since the Leyland TD1 Titans of 1931. There were 24 of them, and they, too, were rebodied: in 1951/52 by Willowbrook, as lowbridge 53-seaters. Originally numbered 816-827 and 884-895, they were renumbered on rebodying as 400-423. Number **414** (**JA7786**) was at Lower Mosley Street, Manchester, in May 1952, on the 64-minute service 6 run to Glossop via Ashton and Stalybridge.

*Below:* The war brought the inevitable Guy Arab utilities, bodied in North Western's case by Roe or Strachan. Most of them were rebodied, again by Willowbrook. Number **24** (**BJA109**) was a 1945 delivery. The rebodying took place in 1950. The new combination was photographed at Piccadilly Gardens, Manchester in May 1952 waiting to leave for Northwich on service 36, a 97-minute journey via Altrincham and Pickmere.

*Above:* In the early postwar period single-decker purchases centred very firmly around the Bristol chassis. No fewer than 40 L5Gs came in 1946, 35 bodied by Brush and the balance by Eastern Coach Works. Number **102** (**BJA402**) was one of the Brush examples, seen in this view at Matlock bus station in July 1953.

*Below:* The next vehicle in the numbering sequence, No. **103** (**BJA403**), was also at Matlock, in this case just over two years earlier, in May 1951. It was displaying a blind for Chesterfield. Behind it stands No. **373** (**AJA136**), one of the 1938 L5Gs which were rebodied in the postwar period by Burlingham as 35-seaters. It was on service 116, a local run to what the timetable describes as "Bonsall" and No. 373's blind as "Bonsnall". Geoffrey Atkins was rather fond of crosslit shots and this picture is a good example of his ability to produce an attractive picture involving a less than perfectly angled sun.

*Above:* The postwar Brush rear-entrance body was also used to re-equip a number of prewar chassis. Nineteen-thirty-six's large intake of Bristol JO5Gs, fleet numbers 727-750 and 754-803, originally bodied as 31-seaters by Eastern Coach Works, were all fitted with the new Brush units in 1946. Numbers 779-803 were 35-seaters, the remainder 31. In this interesting view of No. **771 (JA5571)** when brand new, the BRITISH BUSES logo can be seen on the rear panel between the registration-number plate and North Western's own logo encircling the fleet number. *(Senior Transport Archive)*

*Below:* By the mid to late 1950s, the 1946 Brush bodies were worn out, but the Bristol chassis had plenty of life in them. Rebodyings were once more the order of the day, using 1948 Weymann or 1952/53 Willowbrook bodies from prewar Bristols. Number **906 (BJA427)** was one of the Willowbrook recipients; its body came from No. 906 of 1938 whose fleet number it also took over. BJA427 before the rebodying had been fleet number 127. In its new incarnation it was photographed at Lower Mosley Street, Manchester, in June 1958, working on the Limited Stop service to Blackpool. Ribble's Trumpet Street one-bus outstation is behind the wall. Trumpet Street is long gone, but its *alter ego*, Bugle Street, survives close by.

27

<<< *Previous page:* The Eastern Coach Works version of the postwar Bristol L5G is represented by 1947's No. **148** (**BJA448**), seen at The Square, Buxton in September of that year.

*Above:* In 1947 some second-hand Bristols were acquired from East Midland Motor Services. **ERR602** was numbered 658 on acquisition, but was renumbered **322** upon being rebodied by Burlingham in 1950. This August 1951 picture in The Square, Buxton, rather appropriately has the bus alongside an East Midland vehicle. On the right of the picture is No. **799** (**JA5599**), another of the Brush-rebodied prewar Bristol Js.

*Below:* Number **145** (**BJA445**) is ready to leave for Manchester from Buxton on service 27, whereas No. **151** (**CDB151**) has just arrived from Manchester on the same service. Both buses were 1947 Eastern Coach Works-bodied Bristol L5Gs. The livery variation is noteworthy: No. 145 was in the then new standard livery.

>> *Opposite page:* Number **170** (**CDB170**), another of the 1947 Eastern Coach Works 35-seaters, at Matlock bus station in May 1955, also illustrates the new standard livery adopted at about that time.

29

*Above:* Leyland double-deckers arrived in 1948 after Bristols were no longer available to North Western, starting with ten PD1A Titans fitted with Eastern Coach Works lowbridge 53-seat bodywork. Number **221 (CDB221)**, one of a batch of ten, was at Piccadilly Gardens, Manchester, in May 1952. It was on the 23 to Flixton (Red Lion) via Davyhulme. The blind gave only "RED LION" as the destination: all right for the locals, perhaps, but strangers might well have thought the destination rather vaguely described.

*Below:* "Hayfield via Stockport and Marple" was a less ambiguous legend for service 28. The display was on No. **233 (CDB233)**, one of a batch of 14 PD2/1 Titans with Leyland lowbridge bodywork, also seating 53, which followed the ECW PD1As into the fleet in 1948. A similar vehicle, No. 224, survives in preservation.

*Above:* Some of 1949's PD2/1 Titans were similar to the 1948 batch: standard lowbridge Leyland-bodied 53-seaters, of which No. **242** (**CDB242**), seen at Piccadilly Gardens, Manchester in September 1954, was an example. Its roster has brought it on to service 64 for Styal, though as yet it has no passengers.

*Below:* Six of the 1949 PD2/1 intake were lowbridge 49-seaters with platform doors for longer-distance journeys. Number **248** (**CDB248**) of this version was photographed at the rear of Lower Mosley Street coach station, Manchester, in April 1951. It had run in on service X60 from Blackpool.

>>> *Following page:* A further Titan PD2/1 variation in 1949 was a batch of ten bodied by Weymann as lowbridge 53-seaters. Number **251** (**DDB251**) was in Stockport in April 1954.

*Above:* Nineteen-forty-nine was a busy year for new purchases. Among the most attractive of the year's intake were ten Windover-bodied 32-seat Bristol L5G coaches. Given the very hilly terrain in much of North Western's operating area, the use of Gardner five-cylinder engines in coaches was perhaps unusual. The photographer was in Theatre Square in his home town one lovely day in June 1951 when No. **266** (**DDB266**) came through on the service to Manchester, having just left Huntingdon Street bus station.

*Below:* Number **270** (**DDB270**), the last of the batch, was in Matlock bus station in August 1953. The classic lines of the Windover coachwork are perfectly displayed from this angle and in this lighting. The sliding door to the saloon and the driver's windscreen have been left open against the heat of the day.

The same Windover 32-seat coach body appeared on ten Leyland PS2/3 Tigers, also in 1949. One of Geoffrey Atkins's masterly night shots at Huntingdon Street bus station, Nottingham, in October 1953, includes No. **274** (**DDB274**), which has just arrived from Manchester.

In another Nottingham shot, taken in March 1953, Windover-bodied Leyland PS2/3 No. **277** (**DDB277**) is in Parliament Street, on its way to Manchester.

*Above:* Here is the nearside view of the Windover 32-seat coachwork as fitted to North Western's 1949 Leyland PS2/3 Tigers. In a Huntingdon Street, Nottingham, view taken in February 1952, No. **279** (**DDB279**) waits to leave for Manchester.

*Below:* With evidence of the Cheshire salt industry in the background of this picture, thought to be at Northwich, No. **293** (**DDB293**) appears to be on a private hire assignment. The vehicle was a Weymann-bodied 32-seat dual-purpose Bristol L5G, delivered in 1950. Although the negative for this view is a part of Geoffrey Atkins's collection, the photograph was taken by John Henton.

*>> Opposite page:* One of the oddest aspects of North Western's Atkinson Alphas of 1951 was that the driver had no access to his cab other than through the rear passenger-entrance, but NWRCC had no intentions concerning one-man-operation at this time and front entrances caused problems with bus stop sitings. However, all too soon, that philosophy was overtaken by economic necessity. These vehicles were produced in close collaboration with North Western's engineering staff and were meant to fill the void left by North Western's inability to order Bristol underfloor-engined chassis. Number **394** (**EDB321**) was at Lower Mosley Street, Manchester, in May 1952.

There were two of the Atkinson Alphas, described on page 36, in 1951. The year's only other deliveries were two Leyland HR44 Olympics. Whereas the Atkinsons had Weymann 42-seat rear-entrance bodywork involving a cumbersome access to his cab for the driver, the Olympics, which were 44-seaters, had the more convenient front entrance. The first of the pair, No. **396 (EDB323)**, appears in two views at Lower Mosley Street coach station, Manchester, in May 1952. There are conflicting reports of the bodybuilder for these Olympics. They have been quoted as carrying Weymann coachwork, but the photographer noted Metro-Cammell from the plate on the vehicle at the time of these photographs.

*Above:* Further Atkinsons appeared in the North Western fleet in 1952, again Weymann-bodied 42-seaters and again with rear entrances. There were also two of a lightweight version with Willowbrook bodies. Number **511** (**FDB511**) was at Huntingdon Street, Nottingham in August 1953 with the none-too-easy run to Manchester, Lower Mosley Street, ahead of it. Three hours and nineteen minutes were allowed for the journey.

*Below:* In the following year the order for underfloor-engined buses went to Leyland, who supplied a batch of 36 PSU1/13 Royal Tigers fitted with Weymann 44-seat front-entrance bodywork. There had been a total of only 16 Atkinsons, and the manufacturer must have been disappointed to see North Western turn to Leyland, and later to AEC, for subsequent fleets of similar buses purchased with BET's discounts. North Western's Chief Engineer was more than disappointed: he resigned over the issue. Royal Tiger No. **523** (**FDB523**) was photographed in Nottingham in June 1955.

On a misty day in April 1954 at The Square, Buxton, one of the Weymann-bodied Leyland Royal Tigers, No. **548** (**FDB548**), waits to leave for Manchester (L.M.S.) on service 27. The destination did not refer to a London Midland railway station, but rather to Lower Mosley Street coach station.

*Above:* Weymann supplied the bodywork for six Leyland PD2/12 Titans which were delivered in 1953. One of these lowbridge 53-seaters, No. **555** (**FDB555**), is seen in Piccadilly Gardens, Manchester in July 1953. This example of a most attractive chassis/body combination was working North Western's service 52 to Alderley via Cheadle and Wilmslow. The full service extended to Macclesfield, and was one of those worked "by arrangement" with Manchester Corporation.

*Below:* Number **555** was the subject of an unusual experiment when in May 1959 it was fitted with a Ruston and Hornsby air-cooled engine. The conventional radiator was replaced by an aluminium sheet with air-intake slots, of which there were at least three different versions in the six years 555 ran with the air-cooled engine. This Stockport view from a postcard in the photographer's collection was taken by Roy Marshall.

In an attempt to reduce operating costs through reduced weight, various North Western single-deckers were delivered with, or converted to run on, single, rather than the more usual twin, rear wheels. Leyland Olympic No. 396 of 1951 was one, converted in 1953 (it is seen before the conversion, still on its twin wheels, on page 38); 1952's Atkinsons Nos 512 and 513 were delivered with single wheels; 1953's Royal Tiger No. 519 was also thus converted for a short time. From the Company's 1954 intake, AEC Reliance No. **557** (**FDB557**) *(above)* and Leyland Tiger Cub No. **562** (**FDB562**) *(below)* were among eight vehicles to run on single wheels. Both buses had 44-seat front-entrance bodywork by Weymann and were photographed at Lower Mosley Street, Manchester on the same day in September 1954. Although a further 20 Tiger Cubs (577-596) and ten AEC Reliances (616-625) were delivered with single wheels in 1955, the experiment was concluded fairly soon after that and all the buses concerned restored to the more normal specification.

North Western took some examples of the classic design from Burlingham, the Seagull, on Leyland Tiger Cub chassis in the mid 1950s, among which were six in each of 1954 and 1955. Our pictures illustrate one from each of those batches. Number **565** (**FDB565**) *(above)* was at Chesterfield bus station in January 1956; later the same year, in September, 1955's No. **574** (**FDB574**) was spotted *(below)* in London, parked close to Victoria coach station. These vehicles took advantage of an option introduced by Burlingham to supply a larger destination screen with three-track route number provision, not necessarily needed for vehicles spending all or most of their time on private hire work, but useful for such as the North Western vehicles, which frequently operated express services. Number 565 was transferred into North Western's associated Melba Motors fleet in January 1961.

A fine July 1956 Piccadilly Gardens portrait of another of the Weymann-bodied Leyland PD2/12 Titans on service 52 to Alderley. Number **554** (**FDB554**) displays the graceful lines of the Weymann design including the particularly harmonious treatment of the bonnet and driver's cab. Number **552** of the same batch was alongside.

*Above:* A contrast with the misty April 1954 view taken at The Square, Buxton *(see page 40)*, is afforded by this bright, sunny scene at the same place and in the same month but taken two years later. Weymann-bodied 44-seat AEC Reliance No. **558** (**FDB558**), which had been new in 1954, was apparently about to work as far as Stockport, possibly as a short-working duplicate of a service 27 timing to Manchester via the A6. A single-deck Bristol in the background was also displaying Stockport as its destination, together with the route number 27. Perhaps this was a Sunday whose fine weather had persuaded many Stopfordians to visit Buxton.

*Below:* Leyland-bodied Royal Tiger No. **600** (**FDB600**), a centre-entrance 41-seat coach delivered in 1952, was at Derby bus station in November 1953, whilst working an express timing to Manchester.

*Above:* The Leyland-bodied centre-entrance coaches carried several different livery schemes during their North Western service; sometimes these were the standard of the moment, at others experimental. Number **604** (**FDB604**), seen at Huntingdon Street, Nottingham, on a Manchester "for Blackpool" service in April 1956, was painted in the red and cream scheme used in the mid and late 1950s.

*Below:* Number **600** (**FDB600**), in an August 1959 view at Llandudno, displays a variation of the cream livery when compared with the November 1953 view reproduced on page 45. Here, the window surrounds and lower skirt panels are included in the overall cream. The fleetname has also undergone a change to a trendy and not very successful style which involved the writing leaning backwards. By the end, all the coaches in this batch were showing different front-end treatments after collision damage: although they went very well, an ability to stop quickly was not an attribute of the model.

*Above:* A batch of ten Burlingham-bodied 44-seat AEC Reliance service buses added variety to the fleet in 1955. They were delivered with single rear wheels but were converted to twins in October 1955, eight months or so before this June 1956 view of No. **619 (HJA619)** at Knutsford.

*Below:* The Weymann Fanfare coach body was an attractive addition to the scene in the mid 1950s. North Western had the first one, on an AEC Reliance No. 570, which was exhibited at the Commercial Motor Show in 1954. A batch of five joined No. 570 in 1956, and were virtually identical to the Show model. The first of them was No. **626 (KDB626)**, seen here at Glasshouse Street, Nottingham, on private hire work in May 1957. Its driver was enjoying the comfort of a no doubt well-earned rest in the nearside front seat.

Two of the photographer's favourite and most productive spots are illustrated on this page. As a native of Nottingham, Geoffrey Atkins naturally gravitated to Huntingdon Street bus and coach station to observe and photograph the many operators serving the city. The Weymann bodywork being produced for many BET fleets in the mid 1950s - usually to front-entrance 44-seat specification - found particular favour with him and a fine series of portraits resulted. The view above is of a brand new example on North Western's 1956 Leyland Tiger Cub No. **656** (**KDB656**), photographed in March of that year. Only a month later, No. 656 was a little less shiny at The Square, Buxton *(below)*. In both views the vehicle is bound for Manchester and certain roads would be common to both journeys. The service from Nottingham was joint with the Trent Motor Traction Company.

Nineteen-fifty-six's double-deckers were a batch of ten PD2/21 Titans fitted with Weymann lowbridge 58-seat bodywork with platform doors. The styling was very different from that seen on the earlier PD2/12s. Apart from the visual shock of the enclosed radiator, to a style developed for Midland Red, the lines of the new Orion lightweight body were more austere. Number **668 (KDB668)** was at Piccadilly Gardens in July 1956.

A busy scene at Westwood coach park, Scarborough, in August 1957, had at least seven North Western service buses, including half-cab Bristols, on summer holiday work. On the right, No. **690 (KDB690)**, a 1957 Leyland Tiger Cub, was the service car, which would be the last to leave. It was displaying "Rhyl" in its destination screen. This is unlikely to have been accurate: what probably happened was that the blind was turned to the next destination to "Scarborough" on the blind, which was "Rhyl", no doubt as a ploy to prevent over-anxious passengers from boarding before they had been checked in and assigned a seat in a particular vehicle by the North Western inspector and senior conductor, who can be seen conversing immediately to the right of the cast-iron railings. They would leave on the service car after ensuring that no passengers had been left behind in the confusion.

North Western's two subsidiary coach companies, Melba Motors and Altrincham Coachways, were stocked with vehicles from the main fleet's standard batches painted or repainted blue and cream. These views at a gloriously sunny Llandudno in August 1959 are of Burlingham Seagull-bodied Leyland Tiger Cub No. **703** (**LDB703**) *(above)*, dating from 1957, and *(below)* 1959's Harrington-bodied AEC Reliance dual-purpose 41-seater **776** (**LDB776**). The Leyland was transferred into the Melba fleet in March 1958 where it stayed for nine years before returning to the main fleet just before withdrawal from service. The Reliance was new to the subsidiary fleet, being transferred to North Western in March 1961. It ran thus until withdrawal in 1969.

Nineteen-fifty-seven's intake included a batch of 20 dual-purpose 43-seaters bodied by Weymann on AEC Reliance chassis. Forty-three was rather high as a seating capacity for a "dual-purpose" vehicle, a concept suggesting at least a nod towards coach-like standards of comfort. This type of body as a basic service bus normally had 44 seats. The dual-purpose classification was perhaps more normally achieved by fitting 41 seats into the standard bus shell. Space right across the rear was found for seating in this design, however, at the expense of moving the emergency door from the rear to the offside. Number **721** (**LDB721**) *(above)*, at Lower Mosley Street, Manchester, in June 1958 demonstrates the original striking livery of black, cream and red applied to these vehicles. Number **729** (**LDB729**) *(below)*, was at Gwynedd Road, Llandudno in August 1961, after repaint into service bus livery.

A comparison between North Western's service bus and dual-purpose vehicles with Weymann bodywork. AEC Reliance No. **737** (**LDB737**) and Leyland Tiger Cub No. **533** (**FDB533**) were side by side at Lower Mosley Street in June 1958.

*Above:* A further batch of six Weymann Fanfare-bodied AEC Reliance coaches arrived in 1958. Two of them were repainted blue and cream for the Altrincham Coachways fleet and all were later fitted with high-ratio back-axle gearing for use on Britain's expanding motorway network. Number **744 (LDB744)** was always a unit of the main fleet until its withdrawal in 1969. In this August 1962 view it was at Huntingdon Street, Nottingham, bound for Blackpool with every seat apparently full.

*Below:* Dual-purpose 43-seaters in 1960 were built by Willowbrook on both Tiger Cub and Reliance chassis. Ex-807 (**RDB807**) is seen at Matlock bus station after transfer to the Trent Motor Traction Company as fleet number **365** in March 1972. The photograph was taken in the following July.

North Western's long exclusion from the products of the Bristol factory was partly eased when the Bristol Lodekka design was licensed to Dennis Brothers, of Guildford, who built what was effectively a Lodekka for non-state-owned companies. The Dennis Loline had a strong appeal for North Western, who still had some Bristol chassis of prewar origin giving excellent service. By the time of North Western's first order, however, the Mark II version of the Loline was available, and 15 East Lancs-bodied front-entrance 71-seaters arrived in 1960. Number **814** (**RDB814**) was brand new and gleaming at Lower Mosley Street *(above)* in May 1960. It was on service 28 to Hayfield, which always seemed to get new vehicles as soon as they were delivered (the route ran past Head Office!) Number **818** (**RDB818**) *(below)* was equally new, in the same month, working on hire to Trent in Mount Street, Nottingham.

An interesting development for delivery in 1961 was an order for 41-seat dual-purpose vehicles to Alexander's Highway design, mounted on AEC Reliance chassis. The body was a basic service bus shell fitted with coach seating. North Western classed them operationally as coaches until the 1966 season, when they were redesignated "dual-purpose": a move easily accomplished because of their air-operated doors. At that time, the cream coach livery was replaced by a half-and-half red and cream scheme. After the 1968 season they were further reclassified as service buses: a classic case of "cascading". Number **843** (**RDB843**) represents the Alexander vehicles when new. It was *(above)* at Argyle Road, Llandudno in August 1961. Number **837** (**RDB837**) is seen *(below)* at Nottingham in July 1971 on express work to Liverpool, despite then being classed as a service bus.

*Above:* In 1961 eight petrol-engined Bedford SB3s with Duple Super Vega coachwork with either 37 or 41 seats were bought directly by the subsidiary company Altrincham Coachways. UDB101-108 had their own series of fleet numbers (1-8) which were not shown on the vehicles. Five of the eight later worked under the Melba Motors fleetname and were transferred to the main North Western fleet in March 1967. The whole batch was renumbered 991-998 in 1964. On the original of this print, the fleet number **995** is clearly visible just below the nearside flashing indicator lamp on **UDB105**, thus confounding reports that these fleet numbers were not carried on the vehicles. The picture was taken at Blackpool in May 1967. Later that year all eight were withdrawn.

*Below:* The design of Alexander bodywork on the 1961 AEC Reliances *(see page 56)* was used as the basis for the first North Western 36ft-long coaches in 1962. A batch of ten numbered 907-916 were also the first Leyland Leopard chassis in the fleet. Number **910** (**VDB910**) was at Digbeth coach station, Birmingham in August 1962.

*Above:* In 1963 some 36ft-long Willowbrook-bodied AEC Reliance buses arrived: some had 51 seats and some 53. Number **931** (**VDB931**), one of the 53-seaters, was at Lower Mosley Street, Manchester, waiting to leave on service 27 to Buxton, in May 1965.

*Below:* The 1962 Leopards were 49-seaters in a service bus shell with air-operated doors and were regarded as coaches. The coach/dual-purpose distinction was at this time rather blurred. 1963's Alexander-bodied 49-seaters introduced the Y-type body to the North Western fleet. The shell, with its long, non-opening windows, was clearly more "coach" than "bus", yet the doors were air-operated. The vehicles exactly matched North Western's requirements for express use and became the standard until the demise of North Western as a separate company. In its first summer of service, No. **953** (**VDB953**) was leaving Birmingham's Digbeth coach station heading for the Capital.

>> *Opposite page:* Both types of Alexander-bodied express vehicle were caught side by side in this August 1963 view at Birmingham Digbeth.

*Above:* Rear-engined double-deckers had been available from 1959 but North Western, as we have seen, ordered Dennis Loline IIs in 1960. Mark III Lolines came in 1961 and 1962, but in 1963 the Company decided to split its double-deck requirements between AEC's Renown, bodied by Park Royal as 74-seaters, and 75-seat Alexander-bodied Daimler Fleetlines. There were respectively 18 and 20, and the Renown was operationally the Loline's equivalent. Number **966** (**VDB966**) was at Lower Mosley Street, Manchester, in May 1964.

*Below:* The Fleetline broke new ground for double-deckers. The batch of 20 carried fleet numbers between 1 and 21. Because the Company could not obtain the registration number YJA7, they accepted YJA1-6 and 8-21, leaving the fleet number 7 unused. Number **10** (**YJA10**) was at Lower Mosley Street on the same day. Both these vehicles conformed to the North Western low-height norm. The Company never operated full-height double-deckers in passenger service. The first such vehicle in the fleet was an Eastern Coach Works-bodied machine ex-Rochdale Corporation, which was used as a staff canteen.

*Above:* Further AEC Renowns appeared in 1964, as well as more Fleetlines. The AECs were North Western's last traditional, front-engined double-deckers. Number **120** (**AJA120B**) was at Lower Mosley Street in August 1965. All this batch passed to SELNEC in 1972 and several later worked for a Stevenage, Hertfordshire, independent, where the writer, then living in Stevenage and supplementing his income with some part-time driving, encountered them. AJA120B was often driven, sometimes as far as Clacton, and is recalled as a smooth, reliable vehicle. *Below:* North Western's service 98 passed underneath the Bridgewater Canal by means of a bridge with a headroom of 8ft 9ins. Vehicles built to fit the space available were needed and in 1964 a batch of ten appropriately profiled Strachan-bodied Bedford VAL14s entered service. The quite remarkable thing about this May 1967 view of No. **134** (**AJA134B**) is that it is at Blackpool on the 2hrs 35mins X36 from Sharston.

As the 1960s progressed, coachbuilders really got to grips with the longer coaches by then permitted and some well-thought-out designs appeared from the major and some of the minor coach factories. Though scarcely deserving of the epithet "minor", Harrington nonetheless had not the market penetration of either Duple or Plaxton, despite its Grenadier design being among the most attractive and functional of those available. North Western bought five 32ft-long 41-seat Leyland Leopards thus equipped, of which No. **150 (AJA150B)** is seen *(above)* at Huntingdon Street, Nottingham on an express service to Liverpool in August 1968. It had taken 31 years for a direct service from Nottingham to Liverpool to return *(see page 15)*, this time routed via Derby, Macclesfield and Knutsford instead of Buxton and Manchester. These vehicles were intended mainly for private hire work (despite the above picture), as were a batch of five Duple Northern-bodied Leopards, also 32ft long and seating 41, which came in 1966. Number **228 (FJA228D)**, apparently on private hire work, was at Victoria coach station *(below)* in September 1966.

*Above:* Having been deprived of new Bristol chassis for two decades, North Western was able finally to place an order when in 1968 the *marque* became once more available, as a consequence of Leyland acquiring a stake in Bristol, to non-state-owned purchasers. The short version of the rear-engined Bristol RE, the RESL6G, was chosen, and Marshall, of Cambridge, was awarded the contract to build the 45-seat bus bodies. No fewer than 40 were ordered, presumably in the belief that they would be as reliable and trouble-free as had been the much simpler and more rugged L and K types of an earlier generation. It is probably fair to say that they were not, though like was not being compared with like, for the RE was a vastly more complicated and sophisticated vehicle than had been the earlier types. Number **276 (KJA276F)** is seen at Lower Mosley Street in April 1968.
*Below:* Thirty more Bristol REs came in 1969. These were the longer RELL6G version and had Alexander 49-seat bus bodywork. In a May 1970 view, again at Lower Mosley Street, No. **329 (NJA329H)** was waiting to leave on the X12 over the Pennines to Bradford.

*Above:* Bristol did not have it all its own way, for Leylands were also ordered alongside the Bristols in each of the years 1969, 1970 and 1971. These included ten Leyland Leopards with Plaxton's clean, unfussy Elite II coachwork, of which brand new No. **372 (SJA372J)** is seen at the head of a monumental traffic jam at Haworth, Yorkshire, in May 1971.

*Below:* Although delivered in 1972 to an emasculated North Western, by then headquartered at Wilmslow and solely a coach operator, five Bristol RELH6L coaches (Nos 413-417) with Eastern Coach Works bodies had the traditional North Western red and cream livery: the last new vehicles to be so painted. The move to Wilmslow meant that these coaches were registered by Cheshire County Council rather than Stockport, so No. **413** was registered **JMA413L**. The North Western Road Car Company Limited became extinct on 6th February 1974 when the remnant's identity was changed to National Travel (North West) Limited. The old fleetname was perpetuated, however, as a secondary identity, albeit on all-white National-liveried coaches, until 1977. Number 413, by then thus attired, was at Llandudno in September 1974.